What is a Democracy?
US Government Textbook
Children's Government Books

BABY PROFESSOR
EDUCATION KIDS

Speedy Publishing LLC

40 E. Main St. #1156

Newark, DE 19711

www.speedypublishing.com

Copyright 2017

Have you wondered what a democracy is?

It is a government run by its people. Each citizen has a vote in how its government is run. This differs from a dictatorship or monarchy where a dictator or king retains all power. Because of the democracy of the United States, you will be able to vote when you turn 18 years of age and have your say about how our government is run. Read further to learn about the different types of democracy, its characteristics, and other interesting facts about it.

How did the term evolve? "Democracy" is derived from the Greek word "demos" meaning "people."

Why is the word democracy not used in the Constitution of the United States?

Does this surprise you? The word "democracy" is not used in the U.S. Constitution or the Declaration of Independence. You might think that since the United States is considered a democracy, that this word would be found in either of these founding documents.

JAMES MADISON

First of all, our founders were afraid of the democratic rule. James Madison stated that "...instability, injustice, and confusion ...have in truth been the mortal disease under which popular governments everywhere perished...". In the latter part of the 18th century, being governed by the people was believed to result in disruption and disorder. But they felt that this type of government was superior to Europe's monarchies.

Democracy comes in the form of several sizes and shapes as reflected in the different responses when questions arise about when, how, and to what people are given the power. While it is not used in the Constitution nor the Declaration of Independence, it clearly links to the "rule of law" with a basic principle and shapes American government in a profound way.

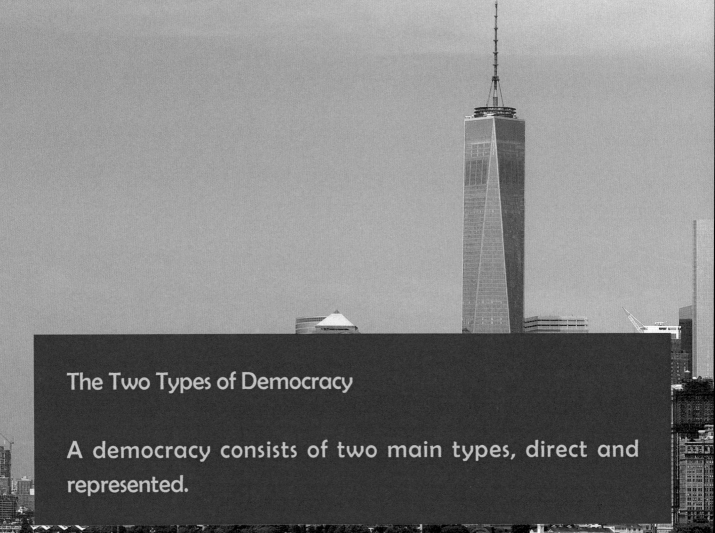

The Two Types of Democracy

A democracy consists of two main types, direct and represented.

A direct democracy states that each citizen has the right to vote on every important decision. One of the first ones democratic votes took place in Athens, Greece. All citizens would gather in the main square and vote on key issues. As the population continues to grow, this becomes difficult. Can you imagine the people in the United States attempting to congregate in one area to vote? This would not turn out well. This is sometimes referred to as a "pure democracy". It is a form where all policies and laws directed by the government are determined by the citizens rather than the elected representatives.

In a true direct democracy, the citizens vote on all bills, laws and even court decisions.

This is opposite to the more common "representative democracy," under which the representatives are elected by the people and are empowered to make policies and laws.

Ideally, the laws and policies enacted by the elected representatives should closely reflect the will of the people's majority.

Ballot referendums and initiatives make it possible for the citizens to put in place, by petition, spending measures or laws that typically might be considered by local or statewide ballots or local and state legislature. Through successful referendums and initiatives, citizens have the power to create, to amend, or to repeal laws, and can also amend local charters and state constitutions.

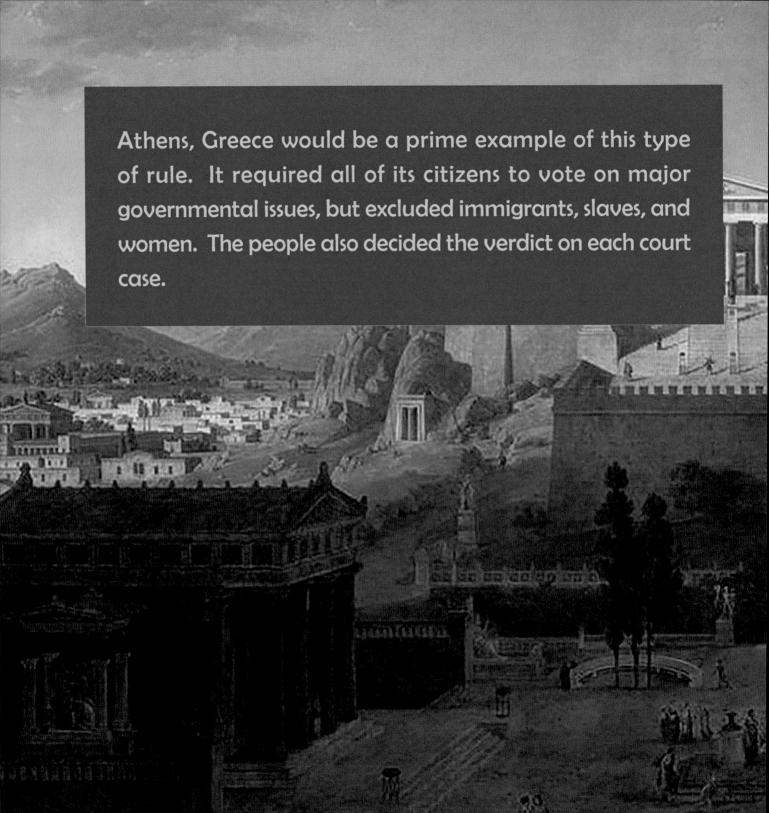

Athens, Greece would be a prime example of this type of rule. It required all of its citizens to vote on major governmental issues, but excluded immigrants, slaves, and women. The people also decided the verdict on each court case.

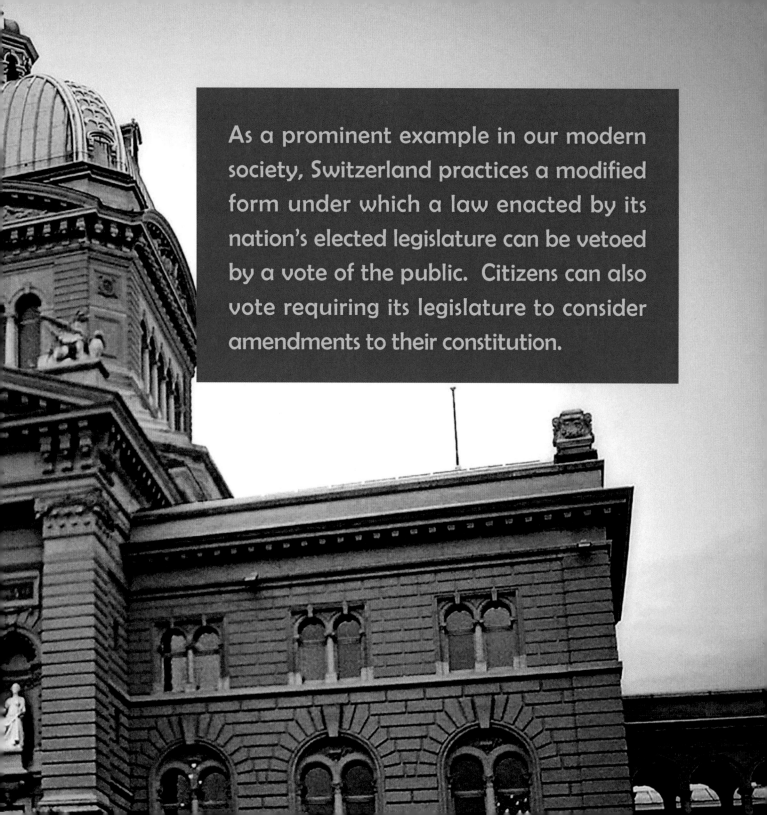

As a prominent example in our modern society, Switzerland practices a modified form under which a law enacted by its nation's elected legislature can be vetoed by a vote of the public. Citizens can also vote requiring its legislature to consider amendments to their constitution.

The other type is a representative democracy. This occurs when the citizens elect their representatives to oversee the government. The United States is an example of a representative democracy. We elect our representatives, including our presidents, senators, and members of congress to oversee the government.

The representatives are elected by the people, similar to the elections for the legislature. These representatives then have authority to choose other representatives, the president, and other officers, the Prime Minister in the last case, which is considered indirect representation.

This power is typically restricted by the constitution, known as a constitutional monarchy or constitutional democracy, or similar measures taken to balance its power.

* An independent judiciary may have power to proclaim legislative acts as being unconstitutional (e.g. supreme court or constitutional court).
* In addition, a constitution can provide deliberative democracy (Royal Commissions) or a direct popular measure (recall elections, referendum, initiative, referendum). However, these may entail legislative action and are not binding. The representatives hold this power.
* Sometimes, a bicameral legislature may have an upper house which is not elected directly. The Canada Senate was modeled after the British House of Lords.

What are its characteristics?

The common characteristics of a democracy are:

Citizens rule – This was discussed earlier under the definition of democracy. The government's power rests in the hands of its citizens either by the election of representatives or directly.

Free elections – This occurs when they conduct fair and free elections and all citizens are permitted to vote as they want.

Majority rule with Individual rights – The majority of the people rule, however their rights remain protected. Each citizen has undeniable rights, including freedom of religion, protection under the law, and free speech.

Limitations on Lawmakers — Certain limits are placed on elected officials, including the president and congress. They are given certain powers and the amount of time they may remain in office is limited.

Citizen participation – In order for this to work, all citizens have to participate. They need to understand the issues presented and they need to vote. Generally, all citizens have the right to vote. In the past, there had been restrictions on wealth, race, or gender, but that is no longer the case.

Reality

Even though is sounds like the perfect form, in reality, there are issues. Some of these criticisms include:

*   Since it is only feasible for the wealthy to run for an office, this leaves the power at the hands of rich.
*   Voters may be uninformed and do not comprehend what the issue is that they are voting for.
*   Voters may have few choices on the issues under a two party system. The United States is a two party system.
*   The large bureaucracy might be inefficient and it can take a long time for decisions to be made.
*   Corruption within the government might limit the fairness of the elections and the power retained by the people.

Despite these issues, however, it has been proven to be one of the most efficient and fair forms of government in today's world. People that live in this type of government tend to have more protections, more freedoms, and a better living standard than in different types of government.

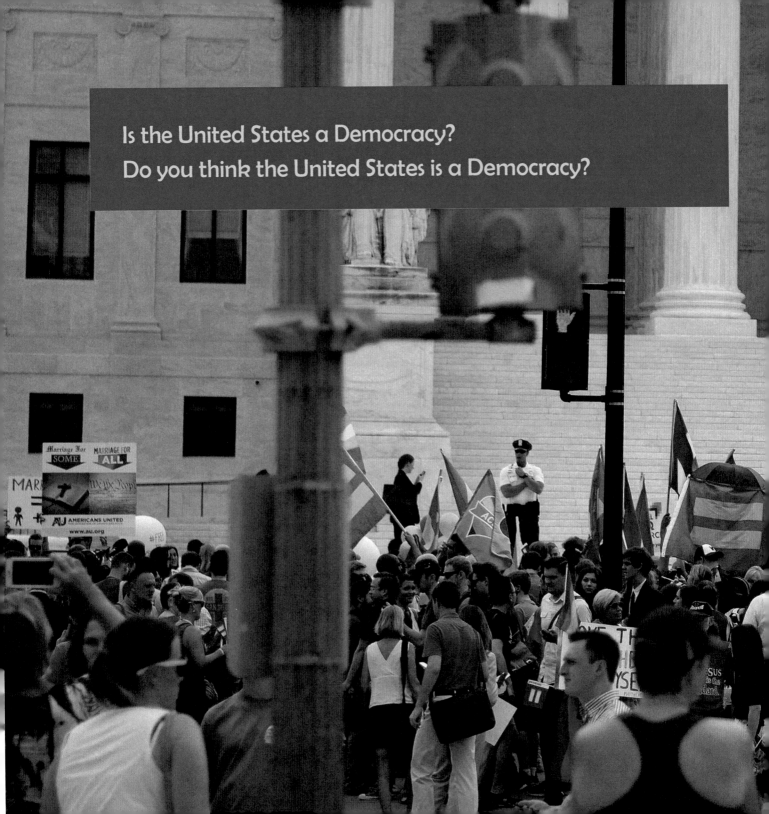

Is the United States a Democracy?
Do you think the United States is a Democracy?

The United States is considered a republic or an indirect democracy. As each citizen may have only a small say, they do have some say in who oversees the government and how it is run.

Think about reciting the Pledge of Allegiance. It contains the following phrase: "and to the republic for which it stands"

Democracy defined is a government form where its people make decisions about policies directly by voting on referendums and initiatives. Furthermore, a republic is a form of government where its people elect representatives who then have the power to decide on policies on behalf of them. The writers of the Constitution feared democracy in its pure form. All that they had studied led them to believe that the they "have ever been spectacles of turbulence and contention; have ever been found incompatible with personal security or the rights of property; and have in general been as short in their lives as they have been violent in their deaths".

In its popular form, the term "democracy" would come to be known as a government form where it obtains its power from its people and then becomes responsible to them in using this power. This might lead you to believe that the United States is a democracy. There are, however, some examples of this type of democracy in action in the United States today that might upset the writers of the Constitution if they were alive.

What Other Countries have Democratic Government?

There are many countries that have a democratic government, but they may be under a different form. Italy, Ireland, India, Germany, and France are considered constitutional republics. Canada, the Netherlands, Spain, the United Kingdom, and Japan are considered as constitutional monarchies. Mexico, Brazil, Argentina, and the United States have a presidential system. France uses a semi-presidential system, whereas, the United Kingdom, the Netherlands, Poland, New Zealand, Italy, Pakistan, India, and Canada use a parliamentary system.

The oldest accepted democracy of the world is the United States.

Made in the USA
Monee, IL
03 February 2024